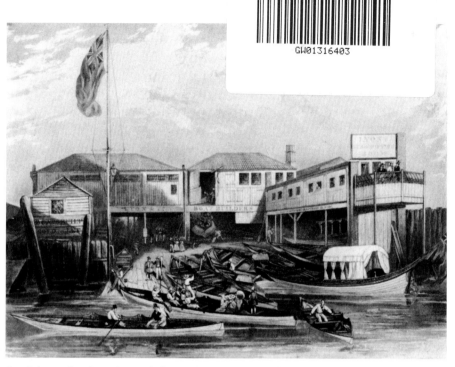

Lyon's boatyard at the southern end of Westminster Bridge specialised in building pleasure craft for rowing and sailing. The broad-beamed boats were rowed by liveried employees of their owners, some shown wearing top hats. (Aquatint after E. F. Lambert.)

The Victorian and Edwardian Sportsman

Richard Tames

A Shire book

CONTENTS

A sporting record 3
Regency roots 5
From rough to respectable 11
Mobility and technology 18
Codes, clubs, competitions and class 21
Playing the game 27
Sport for all? 30
The sporting setting 35
The Olympic ideal 39
Further reading 40
Places to visit 40

Front cover: *The fourth Lord Harris (1851–1932) not only held high government office but also was one of the leading cricketers of his day. He captained Eton, Oxford University, Kent and England and took four wickets in his final match – at the age of seventy-seven. His family home was Belmont, near Faversham in Kent, and the historic cricket field there, where he played many matches, was restored between 2003 and 2007 and is again in use for cricket matches. (Photograph © Trustees of the Harris (Belmont) Charity; website: www.belmont-house.org)*

ACKNOWLEDGEMENTS
The photographs on pages 9 (centre), 24 (top left) and 28 (top) are by Cadbury Lamb; that on page 13 (bottom) is by Richard Tames. The picture on the front cover is reproduced by kind permission of the Trustees of the Harris (Belmont) Charity.

British Library Cataloguing in Publication Data: Tames, Richard. The Victorian and Edwardian sportsman. - (Shire album; 460) 1. Sports - Great Britain - History - 19th century I. Title 796'.0941'09034. ISBN-13: 978 0 7478 0666 0.

Published in 2007 by Shire Publications Ltd, Cromwell House, Church Street, Princes Risborough, Buckinghamshire HP27 9AA, UK. (Website: www.shirebooks.co.uk)
Copyright © 2007 by Richard Tames. First published 2007. Shire Album 460. ISBN 978 0 7478 0666 0.
Richard Tames is hereby identified as the author of this work in accordance with Section 77 of the Copyright, Designs and Patents Act 1988.
All rights reserved. No part of this publication may be reproduced or transmitted in any form or by any means, electronic or mechanical, including photocopy, recording, or any information storage and retrieval system, without permission in writing from the publishers.

Printed in Malta by Gutenberg Press Ltd, Gudja Road, Tarxien PLA 19, Malta.

A SPORTING RECORD

The major features of the British sporting calendar – the Football League and the FA Cup, county cricket and Test Matches, Wimbledon, the Boat Race and the Grand National, regattas at Henley and Cowes, shooting at Bisley – all date from the 'long nineteenth century' that ended with the First World War. 'Muscular Christianity', the Queensberry Rules and the 'Corinthian spirit' epitomised a philosophy of manly striving tempered by self-discipline, generosity towards an adversary and graciousness in defeat. The revival of the Olympic Games was not a British initiative but it was inspired by admiration for the British cult, not of sport, but of *sportsmanship*.

Britons invented tennis, rugby, squash, table-tennis, badminton, netball, water-polo and competitive diving; reformed, regularised and updated horse-racing, archery, boxing, bowls, football, athletics, angling and weightlifting; and imported croquet, polo, snooker, gymnastics, cycling, roller-skating, lacrosse and canoeing. The world's first national athletics championship meeting was organised by the Amateur Athletic Club in 1866. The first competitive show-jumping event was held at the Agricultural Hall, Islington, in 1869. Britain also staged the first international events in water-polo (1890), weightlifting (1891) and clay-pigeon shooting (1893). In 1893 Scotland inaugurated the first national stadium at Hampden, then known more deferentially as Queen's Park. In 1907 Brooklands in Surrey was opened as the world's first purpose-built motor-racing

An interest in archery was revived by the formation of the Toxophilite Society in 1781. The insouciant patronage of the Prince Regent made the sport fashionable among the social elite. As this illustration of 1870 shows, archery was also compatible with voluminous and constricting clothing.

A shooting party in the Highlands. With the advent of railways, the Scottish wilderness became more accessible than ever before, and its adoption by the Royal Family as a preferred holiday destination made it highly fashionable. As foxhunting became more affordable for the middle classes, shooting became increasingly exclusive and ritualised, a sport for the super-rich, who could command remote locations and the services of small armies of ghillies and beaters.

track. In 1908 the first purpose-built Olympic stadium was opened at the White City, Shepherd's Bush, in west London.

Although during the Victorian era such sports as rowing, shooting and yachting became the prerogative of the wealthy few, sport also became a central element in the cultural and social life of the masses, and women participated on an unprecedented scale. More than any other single country, Britain contributed to making sport a codified, competitive and international phenomenon. In doing so it also significantly defined itself as a nation. Gymnastics was for Germans. Training was for Americans. The British *played.*

Inmates of the Fleet Prison while away their ample leisure hours playing rackets against the wall of their prison yard. Note the skittle alley at the bottom left of the picture. (Aquatint after Augustus Charles Pugin and Thomas Rowlandson.)

REGENCY ROOTS

Sport in the Regency period was marked by its brutality, informality, spontaneity, seasonality, regionality and frequent association with gambling, drunkenness and disorder. Apart from an outpost for exiles at Blackheath, golf was confined to Scotland, alongside such other local passions as curling, bowls and the unique contests peculiar to the 'Games' meetings of the Highlands and the Borders. The Lake District and Lancashire had their own particular styles of wrestling. In the West Country the passion was for skittles. Welsh miners favoured rounders, quoits and handball. Northumbrian pitmen bowled heavy iron balls along country roads and gambled on dog-racing or 'coursing' rabbits, a form of hunting guided by sight, not scent. Rowing races between professional watermen reflected a keen rivalry between Thames and Tyne. Speed skating and a form of ice-hockey, known as 'bandy', were to be encountered in the Fenlands.

Knur and spell was a northern (especially Yorkshire) pastime, also referred to as 'poor man's golf'. The player (known as the 'laiker' or 'tipper') aims to launch the knur (ball) from a spring trap (spell) and strike it as far as possible in an agreed number of strokes. (From G. Walker, 'Costume of Yorkshire', 1814.)

Rules for hare-coursing with greyhounds were first drawn up by the Earl of Suffolk on the orders of Elizabeth I. The sport's premier event, the Waterloo Cup, was established in 1836. Drawing crowds of up to 75,000, it was held at Altcar, near Liverpool, on the estate of the Earl of Sefton, shown to the right with his guests, three more earls and a marquis. The meeting of 1840, here depicted, was painted by a locally born protégé of Sefton, Richard Ansdell RA (1815–85), who would specialise in animal painting and eventually accumulate a personal fortune of £50,000.

The greatest sporting craze of the day was 'pedestrianism', the undertaking of epic endurance walks for large wagers or cash prizes. In 1809 at Newmarket Heath Robert Barclay Allardice (1779–1854), also known as 'Captain Barclay', walked 1000 miles in 1000 hours. In 1822 56-year-old George Wilson, sustained by mutton chops and warm gin, walked 90 miles through the foulest weather in 23 hours 46 minutes, on Newcastle's Town Moor, before a crowd of forty thousand.

Animal baiting in various forms retained an enthusiastic following. As late as 1816 there was still bull-running through the streets of Bethnal Green. The Black Country was the heartland of dog-fighting, as the Lake District was of cock-fighting. In the Midlands and East Anglia foxhunting was in its heyday, embracing both peer and

The Royal Cockpit in Westminster, as depicted by Thomas Rowlandson in 1808. London's last legal cock-fighting venue, it was closed in 1825.

A bowling green in the garden of a public house in 1825. Note the number of flagons and glasses. (From B. Blackmantle, 'The English Spy', 1825.

peasant. Hare-coursing also enjoyed aristocratic patronage but shooting was already becoming increasingly exclusive and ritualised as landowners invested heavily in game preservation and the employment of permanent keepers and fearsome mantraps to protect their preserves from poachers. Contemporaries noted the decline of traditional rural pastimes, blaming the enclosure of village commons and, in the south of England especially, the oppression of agricultural labourers, forced to work longer hours and a six-day week on a miserable diet. The accelerating pace of urban life was reflected in a dramatic fall in public holidays. In 1825 the Bank of England closed for forty holidays, in 1834 for four.

Although most of the nation's more than one hundred racecourses held only a single annual meeting, horse-racing was the best organised sport, with Royal Ascot (1711), the *Racing Calendar* (1727), Tattersall's bloodstock auction house (1766), the Oaks (1779) and the Derby (1780) all firmly established. The first point-to-point race was recorded in 1836, organised by the Worcestershire Hunt. Although it attracted an abundance of riff-raff, the Turf

Before the advent of railways made it possible to transport racehorses cheaply over long distances, race meetings were brief, local affairs, largely for the amusement of local gentry. Note that this Norfolk meeting was accompanied by theatrical performances and a cricket match.

7

Sir Tatton Sykes (1772–1863) leading the winner of the 1846 St Leger, named 'Sir Tatton Sykes' in his honour. Sykes was the archetypal bluff Yorkshire patriarch, open-handedly generous in his hospitality to all classes but a domestic tyrant to his own family. In his youth Sykes trained as a bare-knuckle boxer with Belcher, then served as master of foxhounds for forty years and built up a stud of three hundred thoroughbreds.

had since 1752 been under the control of the elitist Jockey Club and the respectable classes used elaborate stands not just for shelter but as a social refuge. The sport was justly characterised by William Cobbett as 'very plebeian and very patrician'.

Cricket, played on country-house lawns as well as village greens, had yet to attain its status as the game that epitomised Englishness and still had a strong regional bias to the south-east, with the most clubs established in Kent (159), Sussex (109), Hampshire (88) and Essex (86). The first Eton v Harrow match was played in 1805, the first Gentlemen v Players match in 1806. Thomas Lord's ground found its third and final home at St John's Wood in 1814. The first cricket club to be permanently established on a county basis was Sussex in 1839. Surrey settled at The Oval in 1845. The first cricket scoreboard was installed at Lord's in 1846.

Boxing, still almost exclusively English, had produced the first sporting superstar. Born in Aldgate, Daniel Mendoza (1764–1836) composed the pioneer 'scientific' treatise on *The Art of Boxing* (1789), stressing the significance of balance over strength and even

Although duelling was frowned on, the ability to fence competently was still regarded as a mark of gentlemanly status. The academy founded by the Italian master Domenico Angelo had passed to his Eton-educated son Henry. Henry shared his Bond Street premises with the prizefighter 'Gentleman' Jackson (1769–1845), who had defeated Mendoza to become English champion. Byron was among his pupils. This illustration of 1821 shows Tom and Jerry, the heroes of Pierce Egan's 'Life in London' (1821), receiving instruction. Tom and Jerry's louche adventures became a literary phenomenon, inspiring dozens of stage adaptations.

Right: *Tom Cribb (1781–1848) demolishing Tom Molineaux in 1811. Molineaux's second was another famous black American pugilist, Bill Richmond. A Bristolian by birth, Cribb became a London coal-porter and was known as the Black Diamond. Molineaux died destitute, of drink, in Ireland.*

Left: *The imposing grave of the boxer Tom Cribb at Woolwich. The Tom Cribb public house in Panton Street, off Leicester Square, also commemorates its sometime proprietor. Having achieved the ambition of many sportsmen in retiring to run a pub, Cribb lost it through betting on horses.*

Below: *Sparring at the Fives Court, James Street, Haymarket. Pugilists Randall and Turner are shown wearing gloves. Known as 'mufflers', these were worn only for practice or exhibition bouts. Real contests continued to be fought with bare knuckles until the publication of the Queensberry Rules in 1867. The all-male gathering represents what was collectively known as 'the Fancy', whose membership ranged from young toffs through army officers to professional coachmen, apprentices and criminal riff-raff. Note the black boxer in the foreground, possibly Tom Molineaux, a former Virginia slave who came to London as a sailor. (Aquatint after T. Blake.)*

The artist James Pollard (1792–1867) sorting and counting the day's bag with his son and a friend (1846). Although he lived most of his life in the new suburb of Islington, Pollard specialised in painting scenes of the field sports that were his own favourite recreation.

speed. Never more than 160 pounds (73 kg) in weight and 5 feet 6 inches (168 cm) in height, 'Mendoza the Jew' became champion of all England, retiring to run a celebrated boxing academy. Huge sums changed hands on the outcome of fights. As the patron of Tom Cribb, Captain Barclay won £10,000 when Cribb beat the former American slave Tom Molineaux in twenty minutes before a crowd of twenty thousand in rural Leicestershire. How, before the advent of railways, such huge numbers regularly assembled in remote areas to watch prize fights – which were illegal – remains a puzzle.

Like racing, boxing enjoyed the support of both the highest and the lowest, a motley following known collectively as 'the Fancy', whose chronicler, the pioneer of sporting journalism, was Pierce Egan (1772–1849). Egan's status as the doyen of an emerging profession was established in 1812 with the publication of *Boxiana, or, Sketches of ancient and modern pugilism, from the days of the renowned Broughton and Slack to the heroes of the present milling era.* Travelling widely to cover hunts, prize fights and race meetings, Egan described sporting encounters and personalities in a racy, florid slang in which eyes invariably became 'peepers' and blood 'claret'. *Pierce Egan's Life in London and Sporting Guide,* first published in 1823, merged with the recently established *Bell's Life in London* to become *Bell's Life,* Britain's main sporting journal for the next half century.

Parallel with the emergence of a sporting press and sporting literature was the growing popularity of the sporting print, a speciality of the Alken family, most notably of Henry Thomas Alken (1785–1851), whose *National Sports of Great Britain* (1820) featured hunting, racing and shooting.

FROM ROUGH TO RESPECTABLE

The nineteenth-century revolution in society's attitude to sport was part of the broader concern of Quakers, Wesleyans and Evangelicals to promote sobriety, orderliness and compassion in a movement embracing prison reform, Sunday Schools, the abolition of the slave trade and child labour, the provision of professional police and 'rational recreation' through public parks, libraries, galleries and museums. The foundation of the (later Royal) Society for the Prevention of Cruelty to Animals was followed by the closure of London's last cockpit (1825) and, after a 35-year campaign and the introduction of no less than eleven parliamentary bills, the banning by statute of baiting bulls and other animals (1835). Despite this, cock-fighting, dog-fighting and ratting continued, especially in remote rural areas, where magistrates themselves might turn a blind eye or even participate. Throughout the century efforts would be made repeatedly to dissociate sport from its traditional accompaniments – drink and gambling – and to purge competitive occasions of the taint of nobbling, unfair play and rowdiness. To the extent that these efforts succeeded – as they did in such previously tainted sports as racing, boxing and athletics – the sportsman came increasingly to embody what were held to be not only the finest but the defining qualities of the British character.

It is perhaps significant that the first historian of cricket was a clergyman, the Reverend James Pycroft (1813–95), who praised the game as an instrument of moral

After the banning of cock-fighting in 1849, ratting remained the last legal form of animal baiting, there being little sympathy, even among the tender-hearted, for the victims. A suitable pit could be built cheaply and easily in a back yard or room of a pub. Note the gas lighting and the respectable dress of the crowd shown in this painting of c.1855–60. (The flags and soldiers' uniforms suggest the period of the Crimean War.) Supplying rats at 3d each proved a profitable sideline for the professional rat-catchers, who kept warehouses and homes free of vermin. The journalist Henry Mayhew recorded one London publican buying in 26,000 rats a year. Bets were placed on the number of rats a terrier could despatch within a set time limit. The celebrated 'Billy' once accounted for a hundred in five and a half minutes.

uplift: 'It is no small praise of cricket that it occupies the place of less innocent sports. Drinking, gambling, cudgel-playing insensibly disappear before a manly recreation which draws the labourer from the dark haunts of vice and misery to the open common… Cricket, philosophically considered, is a standing panegyric on the English character; none but an orderly and sensible people would so amuse themselves.'

It was in the reformation of the nation's ancient public schools that the cult of sport most visibly emerged. Rather than being an acknowledged part of the curriculum, sport had traditionally been left for pupils to organise. A form of hockey was known at Eton by 1830 and cross-country running at Shrewsbury by 1831. Occasional contests between rival schools took place at cricket and rowing, sometimes in defiance of headmasters.

Educational reformers argued that sport could be used to channel youthful energies,

Above: 'Foot-ball' – note the hyphenation: the term 'soccer', derived from 'Association' football, was not recorded until 1891. Thomas Webster's painting, first exhibited at the Royal Academy in 1839, was reproduced as a steel engraving in 1864, the year after the formation of the Football Association. It depicts the traditional village game, long played by men as well as boys, in which there was no fixed pitch, no limit on sides and virtually no rules. The artist has taken care to show several boys tumbled over or rubbing injuries. 'Hacking' – deliberately kicking shins – was originally accepted as a legitimate tactic of the game as played by school and university sides but was banned by FA rules.

Below: 'Foot Ball at Rugby', drawn in 1845, depicts a 'skrummage'. Note that all the players wear peaked caps.

Of Flemish descent, Nicholas Wanostrocht (1804–76) inherited a boys' school at Blackheath when he was just nineteen. Wary of the parents' reaction to his devotion to cricket, he adopted the professional pseudonym of Nicholas Felix. A brilliant left-handed bat and cunning bowler, Felix played for over twenty years for Kent and for the Gentlemen versus the Players. A gifted artist, he published in 1845 'Felix on the Bat', the first illustrated book on batting technique, which additionally showed what not to do. Felix also invented the first bowling machine, as well as batting gloves, leg guards, and a peaked cap more practical than the top hat previously worn. In recognition of Felix's contribution to cricket, the MCC organised the first ever Lord's benefit match for an amateur, played in the presence of the Prince Consort.

distract pubescent males from experimentation with drink, tobacco or sex and promote instead the virtues of leadership, loyalty, stamina and self-mastery; as the 1853 Prospectus of the Harrow Philathletic Club asserted, 'The encouragement of innocent amusements and recreation must tend greatly to the maintenance of order and discipline throughout the School'. In *Tom Brown's Schooldays* (1857) Thomas Hughes praises boxing on the grounds that 'there's no exercise in the world so good for the temper'. The 'character-building' value of sport was warmly endorsed by the 1864 Clarendon Commission on public schools as making the nation's elite youth fit 'to govern others and control themselves'. Alongside such ancient foundations as Eton and Winchester, new schools such as Uppingham, Repton,

A proficient oarsman and cricketer, Lord George Bentinck (1802–48) was a brilliant horseman who spent £45,000 a year on a stable of two hundred horses. The 'Napoleon of the Turf' introduced the practice of parading the runners in the paddock before each event, numbering horses to identify them and starting races by lowering a flag. Bentinck also campaigned successfully to confirm the legality of on-course and high-stakes betting, pioneered the use of horse-boxes and founded a benevolent fund for destitute jockeys and trainers.

Marlborough and Loretto became famed for sporting excellence. Through the medium of the boys' boxing club, institutions such as Haileybury and Repton began to offer the slum lads of London's East End a path to self-respect through sport.

Sports played at school were carried on at university and in other institutions where fit young men were congregated. At Oxford, Exeter and Brasenose Colleges were trailblazers in promoting alternatives to the country sports in which undergraduates had conventionally indulged to pass away their afternoons. The first 'Varsity' cricket match was played in 1827. The first Oxford v Cambridge boat race was rowed at Henley in 1829 – for a monetary stake; it became an annual event from 1839. The first athletics contest between the universities took place in 1864. A rugby team is known to have existed at Guy's Hospital by 1843. Self-improving artisans represented another distinct constituency. The Birmingham Athenic Institute was founded in 1842 by Christian Chartists and, alongside evening classes in dancing and elocution, had groups dedicated to cricket, football, quoits, running, jumping and wrestling.

In the armed services sport was increasingly perceived as a useful adjunct to formal arms and foot drill, improving levels of physical fitness, offering an alternative to idleness and alcohol, and enhancing unit cohesion through boxing, fencing and shooting competitions at company, battalion and regimental levels. The building of permanent barracks, as opposed to the traditional practice of billeting soldiers in public houses,

It is doubtful whether the Duke of Wellington did ever claim that the Battle of Waterloo was won on the playing-fields of Eton but the revived public schools of mid-Victorian Britain valued hard-fought team games as the crucible of manhood. In the mid-ground of this depiction of Eton in 1844 is the celebrated wall that provided the focus for the school's unique and – to outsiders – incomprehensible 'wall game'. Note that the bowler is still bowling under-arm. (Lithograph after C. W. Radclyffe.)

made it possible to complement them with sports facilities. A sports day was held at Woolwich Academy for the first time in 1848, and by the Honourable Artillery Company in 1858. An Army Gymnastic Staff, initially of twelve non-commissioned officers, was formed in 1860.

Polo and tent-pegging helped maintain standards of horsemanship and skill with the lance. A mid-century war scare with France led to the establishment of the National Rifle Association in 1859 and the recruitment of Volunteer rifle companies, which brought shooting to Britain's cities on small-bore rifle ranges. The first NRA shooting championships were staged on Wimbledon Common in 1861. Volunteer companies then sought to keep up their membership by offering a range of other sporting activities and facilities. When the youthful Alexander Fleming, future discoverer of penicillin, first came to London he joined a London Scottish rifle company as the fastest way to find fellow Scots.

Perhaps the ultimate endorsement of sport's growing respectability was the involvement and approval of the royal family. The Toxophilite Society (1781) acquired 'Royal' status in 1844, the Canoe Club (1866) in 1873. The Highland Gathering at Braemar near Balmoral also came to enjoy

The popularity of billiards was boosted when Queen Victoria's husband, Prince Albert, became a devotee. Despite the implications of this John Leech cartoon, the game was decidedly a masculine monopoly, with the billiards room serving as an adjunct to the smoking-room as an all-male preserve. The game was brought within reach of the working classes when the larger and more luxurious public houses installed tables.

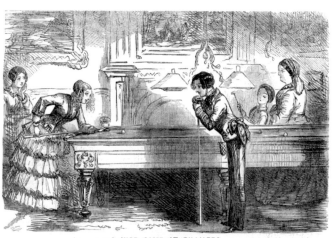

A NICE GAME AT BILLIARDS.

Pretty Cousin. "LET ME SEE, FREDERICK! I'M JUST EIGHTEEN TO YOUR LOVE!"
Frederick (who is always so ridiculous). "THAT IS PRECISELY THE STATE OF THE CASE, MY DEAREST GEORGINA."
Mamma (with severity). "COME! LUNCHEON IS QUITE READY."

The Braemar Gathering, held near the royal retreat at Balmoral, became the most prestigious of a circuit of 'Highland' games at which semi-professional Scottish athletes competed in such unique events as throwing the hammer and tossing the caber. The Fort William gathering included a race up Ben Nevis. All-time champion Donald Dinnie retired in 1910 aged seventy-three, having won eleven thousand events.

Glorious Goodwood in 1885 is notable for the portly presence of the Homburg-hatted, exquisitely tailored Prince of Wales (left centre). The presence of uniformed police guaranteed the exclusivity of the Royal Enclosure. (Detail from an oil painting by J. Walter Wilson and Frank Walton.)

The Prince of Wales shooting at Sandringham in 1893. As riding to hounds became more accessible to urban sportsmen, shooting became increasingly exclusive and expensive, requiring small armies of keepers and beaters to co-ordinate drives of game-birds towards elaborate battues. The Prince, an outstanding shot, is attended by his personal loader and cartridge boy. The inset picture shows him driving to the shoot in a brake. Within a few years he became a fervent fan of the motor-car.

regular royal patronage. Bisley's blue riband trophy was the Sovereign's Prize. The Prince of Wales, athletic in his youth, dabbled with tennis, was an enthusiast of motoring, excelled at shooting game and was an ardent devotee of the Turf, revelling in popular acclaim when his horse, Persimmon, won the Derby, the St Leger and the Ascot Gold Cup. Admittedly none of these activities implied much, if any, direct contact between members of royalty and the common herd. In 1914, however, George V set a precedent by becoming the first British monarch to attend the FA Cup Final.

Railways brought 'coarse fishing' within reach of millions, leading to an increase in the prestige and expense of 'game fishing' for trout or salmon along the increasingly exclusive rivers of Hampshire and Scotland. This John Leech cartoon of 1864 suggests a going rate of £30 a week.

SALMON-FISHING!

Friend (on the bank). "WELL, JACK! HAVE YOU HAD PRETTY GOOD SPORT?"
Jack. "SPORT! IF YOU CALL IT SPORT TO HAVE NO WATER AND NO FISH, AND TO PAY NINETY POUNDS FOR THREE WEEKS OF IT, I'VE HAD PLENTY!"

MOBILITY AND TECHNOLOGY

Marked improvements in standards of road construction and carriage design, followed by the advent of the railways from the 1830s onwards, enlarged the arena of sporting competitiveness from a local to a national scale as school and club teams became able to travel to confront their rivals. Race meetings could now attract contestants from hundreds rather than dozens of miles away. Pigeons could henceforth be transported over similar distances before being released to race back home. The dangerous craze for competitive coach-racing along public roads, which reached a peak of popularity in the 1820s, was, however, killed off in a decade with the demise of the mail-coach.

Railways offered urban sportsmen rapid access to the countryside to take part in foxhunting, angling or point-to-point racing. In 1867 railway companies sponsored publication of *The Rail and the Rod*, identifying angling locations within a 30-mile radius of London. Cheap fares for anglers were introduced in 1872; the chartering of whole trains by clubs soon followed. At the other end of the social scale, Cowes Week would

Regatta Week at Cowes in the 1890s. Note the steam launches, which enabled privileged spectators to keep up with the races.

The touring Australian cricket side of 1893. The opening of the Suez Canal in 1869 and the invention of the steam turbine revolutionised international shipping, making it possible for teams to compete with opponents from the opposite side of the world.

scarcely have attracted the number of females and families that it did had not the Solent become easily accessible from the capital by rail.

Sport, through the garrisoning of imperial outposts and the establishment of emigrant communities, became an aspect of the British civilising mission. As early as 1853, Australian settlers created in Melbourne what was then the world's largest cricket ground. The first touring cricket side to visit England, in 1868, was a team of Australian Aborigines. Mayo College, an elite institution for anglicising the offspring of India's princes, employed no less than five games masters. The opening of the Suez Canal in 1869, coupled with dramatic improvements in the fuel efficiency of steam-powered shipping, made possible a globalisation of sporting competition, culminating in the re-establishment of the Olympic Games in 1896.

In an age of ever advancing industrial progress, no material aspect of British life could remain unaffected. Without the invention of the lawnmower in 1830 it is inconceivable that spin bowling would have developed into a subtle art or that croquet and lawn tennis would have conquered the leafy gardens of suburbia. The first outrigger sculling boat, with a beam of just 12 inches (30 cm), was built in 1845 by Cambridge undergraduates Frederick Furnivall of Trinity Hall and Jack Beesley of St John's College. In the same year a 60 foot (18 metre) outrigger racing eight was built for the Cambridge crew by Searle's in just eight days.

New materials, the products of inventive ingenuity or the exotic imports of a global commerce, such as gutta-percha and rubber, transformed the design and performance of such items as racquets, golf balls and tennis balls. Billiards became far more subtle and precise owing to the replacement of the wooden table bed with slate and the substitution of rubber cushions for the traditional cotton or horsehair ones.

Advances in metallurgy and engineering design, such as the invention of breech loading, produced sporting guns that could fire further and more accurately and be reloaded faster. The clay pigeon, made of river silt and pitch, was invented in 1880, the same year as the mechanised trap for propelling it.

The patenting of a practicable pneumatic tyre in 1888 led to a craze for cycling in the 1890s. By the Edwardian period sophisticated models were available for the children of the affluent middle classes. £10 would represent a month's wages for a skilled artisan.

Football was first played by floodlight at the Bramall Lane ground in Sheffield in 1878 and rugby in the same year at Broughton in Lancashire. The world's earliest known hard tennis court, and the first court in Australia, was laid in asphalt at St Kilda, Melbourne, in the same year.

As rising incomes, shorter working hours and the advent of compulsory schooling combined in the last third of the nineteenth century to promote mass participation in sport, it stimulated the mechanisation of the production of sports equipment and clothing and its distribution through specialist outlets like Lillywhite's or the dedicated departments of family stores such as Gamage's.

The treatment of sports injuries offered a lucrative new market for the emerging pharmaceutical industry, as witnessed by these advertisements for the alleged universal efficacy of Elliman's Embrocation.

CODES, CLUBS, COMPETITIONS AND CLASS

Traditional country pastimes were notable for the simplicity of their rules, which often varied from one county to another. As sports became more complex and were played on a national scale, the need for uniform written codes became apparent. Clubs often became the national ruling authority for a sport as a whole. The earliest surviving written rules for golf were drawn up by the St Andrews club for its first competition in 1754. The Toxophilite Society established the conventions for targets and distances used in competitive archery. As the body responsible for the ancient royal sport of real tennis, the Marylebone Cricket Club (MCC) also issued the first rules for lawn tennis in 1875, although tennis soon became synonymous with the Wimbledon club, as polo did with Hurlingham. Rowing was moulded by the conventions of Henley Royal Regatta. New authorities and clubs came into existence when what had been pastimes sought to regularise themselves as competitive sports, as in the case of swimming (1837), curling (1838), skating (1842) and fencing (1848).

Rule-making was always potentially contentious, risking secessions by partisans of particular traditions or techniques. There was also the question of latitude in matters of detail. The circumference of the cricket ball, for example, was not standardised until 1838, some half a century after its permitted weight had been determined. Round-arm bowling is first recorded in 1807 but did not become mandatory until 1864.

Football, originally an anarchic scrimmage contested between whole villages, with no fixed ground and almost no rules, developed variously at differing public schools. Handling the ball was accepted as lawful in the way the game was played at Rugby School. The first recorded eleven-a-side match took place at Eton in 1841, the two sides being respectively the 'Wet-Bobs' (i.e. those who rowed) and the 'Dry-Bobs' (those who did not). In the same year the first known football club was founded at Caius College, Cambridge. It took the formation of the Football Association (FA) in 1863 to formulate a definitive code which differentiated soccer from the handling game.

The first football tournament, contested in 1868, was for the Yorkshire Football Association's

Steeplechasing became popular in the 1830s, when most races were run over open country according to local rules. The Grand National was first run at Aintree, near Liverpool, in 1839; unusually, the course had a grandstand, although part of it ran over farmland until 1885. The Jockey Club initially shunned steeplechasing on account of the undesirable elements it attracted but in 1866 established the National Hunt Committee to regulate both steeplechasing and hurdle races.

The first hockey club was founded at Blackheath c.1861–2. Rules were refined by the Teddington Club, which introduced the shooting circle, replaced the original rubber cube with a ball and banned the lifting of the stick above shoulder height. The original member clubs of the male-only Hockey Association (1886) were all in the environs of London.

Right: *The All-England Croquet Club, founded at Wimbledon in 1868, organised the first national championships in 1870, as depicted by* The Graphic. *Tennis soon eclipsed croquet at Wimbledon but a separate Croquet Association was formed in 1896 and by 1914 had 170 affiliated clubs.*

Cromwell Cup, won by Sheffield Wednesday. The FA Cup, based on an inter-house knock-out competition at Harrow School, was originally dominated by elite, amateur clubs from the south. In the first final, played at The Oval, Wanderers beat the Royal Engineers 1-0. As late as 1880 the final attracted only four thousand spectators. The turning point came in 1883 when the Old Etonians lost to the professionals of Blackburn

Cowbridge Grammar School football team, 1877. The plain collar-less jersey is complemented by knee-length breeches and knee-high socks. Did they play in the striped pill-box hats?

Famous English footballers, 1881. Caborn (second left), Widdowson, Luntley, Sands and Earp (seated right) wear the plain red shirt of Nottingham Forest. Bailey, Sparks and Prinsep all played for Clapham Rovers. Prinsep had represented England at seventeen, Mosforth at nineteen. Bambridge, a Lloyd's underwriter, played for three different clubs and Sparks for six; both became members of the Football Association committee. Marshall had been a professional sprinter.

Olympic, who, to the undisguised disapproval of their opponents, had spent weeks in training for the contest. A row which might have led to the establishment of rival amateur and professional associations was averted by the London-based FA's acceptance of professionalism in 1885. Even so, the founding members of the Football League, which organised fixtures on a weekly basis, were all based in the industrial cities of the North and Midlands. The first London club to be admitted to the League was Arsenal in 1913.

By 1893 the FA Cup Final attendance was 45,000 and by 1901, when the event was filmed for the first time and Tottenham Hotspur brought the cup back south for the first time since 1882, it was 110,000.

There was a similarly rapid growth in the number of football clubs in England and Wales, from about one thousand in 1888 to over eight thousand by 1900. Liverpool alone had over two hundred, organised in thirteen amateur leagues, recruiting their core membership variously from churches, factories, pubs and neighbourhoods. Aston Villa, Everton, Barnsley, Bolton, Birmingham, Fulham and Wolverhampton Wanderers all originated as church-based teams. Leyton Orient, Tottenham Hotspur and Preston North End grew out of cricket clubs, Brentford from a rowing club. Blackburn was formed by the old boys of the local grammar school. Manchester United owes its origins to men of the Lancashire & Yorkshire Railway. Millwall was formed by workers from Morton's jam factory on the Isle of Dogs, Arsenal from the armaments works at Woolwich and West Ham United at the initiative of the proprietor of the Thames Ironworks, Oxford-educated A. F. Hills (1857–1927). Celtic was formed by Irish Catholics to raise funds for free meals for needy children. Unusually, Chelsea was established as a commercial venture by local businessman H. A. Mears after failing to persuade Fulham to base themselves at the former Stamford Bridge athletics ground.

Below: The route of the Varsity boat race from Mortlake to Putney was finally settled in 1845. By the time of Gustave Doré's engraving, some thirty years later, the 'Boat Race' had become a national institution. It not only drew huge crowds of all classes to the riverside but was followed with passionate interest far beyond the capital or the university cities. 'Boat Race Night' in London became notorious for rowdy behaviour by drunken undergraduates, usually leading to appearances the next day at Bow Street Magistrates' Court.

Above: Last innings: the gravestone of Charles Sheldrick at Sawston in Cambridgeshire asserts an undying allegiance to cricket, if not to any particular club.

'The Derby gives all London an airing, an "outing"; makes a break in our over-worked lives and effects a beneficial commingling of the classes'; so wrote Blanchard Jerrold in the text to accompany Gustave Doré's 'London: A Pilgrimage' (1872).

Bhupendra Singh (1891–1938), Maharajah of Patiala, captained the Indian cricket side that toured England in 1911. A fine shot, he also fathered eighty-eight children before dying of a heart attack playing polo. Introduced from India by cavalrymen, polo spread to the equestrian elites of the United States and Argentina.

The establishment of a separate Scottish Football Association and Scottish League had the doubtless unintentional side-effect of virtually guaranteeing the survival of separate, distinctively Scottish newspapers, a large part of whose readership was primarily interested in coverage of the local sporting scene.

The identity of specific sports clubs became elaborated through the development of individual traditions, ceremonies and eccentricities and signified by an iconography of costume and a liturgy of celebration and commemoration. The Scottish golfers of Blackheath sported a splendid scarlet coat, of military cut, with gold epaulettes, as early as the mid eighteenth century. The earliest recorded badge, worn on the jacket, was adopted by the Duddington Curling Club of Midlothian in 1802. The blazer, as a form of sportswear rather than a naval garment, is first recorded as being worn in 1838 by the Cricket Union of Mexico! The blazer was first adopted in England as sportswear in 1862 by the Lady Margaret Boat Club of St John's College, Cambridge. In 1844 Exeter College Boat Club ordered a special boating handkerchief, probably to be worn round the neck, to be

The Oxford Boat Race crew of 1893. By then, club uniforms had become so de rigeur that undergraduates wore them as regular day clothes, puzzling the aged Gladstone when he revisited Oxford. Oxford won the Boat Race every year from 1890 to 1898. V. Nickalls (front left) was a member of a family of distinguished oarsmen.

Hurdle-racing at Lillie Bridge, Brompton, in 1871. Competitors appear to be wearing identical kit, and the dress of the spectators marks their superior social status. The Mincing Lane Athletic Club, founded by City businessmen in 1863, became the London Athletic Club, which has the longest continuous history of any athletic club. The first Oxford–Cambridge athletics fixture took place in 1864. The Amateur Athletic Association was formed in 1880 to purge the sport of gambling, fixing and rowdiness. Professionals, however, continued to perform for decades, usually to higher standards than amateurs.

available for sale to members only. The earliest known club necktie was being worn by the Eton Ramblers Cricket Club by 1863. International caps for football were introduced by the FA in 1886. The first club colours of which there is certain knowledge were adopted by the celebrated peripatetic cricketing side I Zingari ('The Gypsies') at their inaugural match at Newport Pagnell in 1845. Black, red and gold, they were poetically intended to symbolise ordeal or possibly enlightenment – out of darkness, through fire into light.

PLAYING THE GAME

Working-class incomes began to rise significantly from the 1870s onwards owing to the combined effects of falling food prices, stronger trade unions and rising standards of education. Combined with shorter working hours, this enlarged the potential pool of paying spectators for sport, especially at weekends, in the evenings and on public holidays, leading to the further professionalisation of football and rugby, alongside such already commercialised sports as boxing and racing. This provoked its own reaction. The term 'amateur' first acquired its current connotation of playing for love of a sport rather than monetary reward in the 1880s. The Amateur Boxing Association was founded in 1880. The Amateur Rowing Association, established in 1882, explicitly excluded 'menial and manual workers' from membership, taking its cue from the Amateur Athletic Association, founded in the Randolph Hotel in Oxford in 1866, which had set a precedent of shunning 'mechanics, artisans or labourers'.

When Aston Villa first charged admission in 1874 the gate takings came to 5s 3d (26p); by 1904 they totalled £14,000. Little, however, went the way of the average player. Most 'professionals' were still part-timers with regular, usually artisan, jobs. The Football Association set an annual maximum wage for professional footballers at £208. The limitation was widely evaded in practice by the provision of free housing or additional payments for performing phantom administrative tasks.

The more successful cricketers were earning around £275 a year in the 1890s;

Above: *Prime Minister A. J. Balfour, depicted in this Linley Sambourne cartoon of 1889, was both an accomplished golfer and an ardent tennis player. Churchill, Lloyd George and the Prince of Wales were also regular golfers. A game for all classes in Scotland, golf became virtually a middle-class monopoly south of the border. In newly built suburbs the clubhouse often functioned as a country club.*

Right: *Footballer Alf Common (1880–1946) started his career with Sunderland (1900–1) before transferring to Sheffield United, and scoring their first goal in their 1902 FA Cup victory over Southampton. Common, who made three appearances for England, was one of twelve internationals then playing for United. After another season with Sunderland (1904–5), he went to Middlesbrough in the first transfer deal worth over £1000. After 168 appearances (1905–10), Common moved to Woolwich Arsenal (1910–12) and finished his career with Preston North End (1912–14). He retired to run a pub in Darlington.*

Below: *Fred Archer (1857–86), pictured with his chief patron, Lord Falmouth, was an immensely popular sporting superstar, dogged by private tragedy. The son of a winner of the Grand National, Archer became champion jockey at sixteen and remained so for thirteen successive seasons until his early death, winning twenty-one classic races. Severely depressed by the death of his first child and then of his wife, Archer undermined his constitution with a training diet of castor oil, toast and tea laced with gin, before shooting himself on the second anniversary of his wife's death. He left a fortune of £66,000 and a nation in mourning.*

Above: *The Cricketers inn at Duncton near Petworth in Sussex was once owned by John Wisden and managed by his team-mate James Dean, a Duncton man by birth, co-founder of the United England XI and also Duncton's parish clerk.*

many, however, were simply laid off in the winter and left to support themselves and their families until the next season started. Apart from helping to maintain the grounds, professional cricketers were expected to mend kit, serve drinks to their amateur colleagues and use separate entrances and dressing-rooms. Long-serving professionals might hope for a benefit match after a decade. With luck this might yield up to £1000, enough to start up a sports shop or other small business for retirement.

Rising literacy stimulated the expansion of specialised publications. The *Sporting Press* first appeared in 1853, *The Field* in 1859, the *Sportsman* in 1864 and *Sporting Life* in 1865. By the 1880s *Sporting Life* had a circulation of some 300,000. In 1867 a press box was opened at Lord's, an indication of the increased coverage given to sport in regular newspapers. Sport-specific journals included *Athletic News*, first published in 1875, and *Cricket*, which appeared in 1882.

Wisden's Cricketer's Almanac, the nonpareil of sporting

'The most wonderful cricketer that ever held a bat' – W. G. Grace (1848–1915) in 1877, as captured by 'Spy' (Sir Leslie Ward) for 'Vanity Fair'. Grace made his Lord's debut at sixteen and went on to captain Gloucestershire and England in a career spanning forty-three years. The first cricketer to make a hundred centuries, he also took 2876 wickets while pursuing a parallel career as a parochial doctor to the poor. A committed athlete in his youth, Grace in later life became a keen golfer and also captained the England bowls team in its first international match, against Scotland, in 1903. The lack of a public-school background probably denied him a knighthood; nor did he scruple to benefit financially from his fame.

Jack Hobbs (1882–1963) was the first English cricketer to be knighted. The son of a Cambridge college servant, Hobbs was well served by a calm and reserved demeanour which protected him from the snobberies of the amateur playing elite. Hobbs played for Surrey from 1905 to 1935 and appeared sixty-one times for England, amassing 197 first-class centuries, ninety-eight of them after the age of forty. In retirement he ran a sports goods shop in Fleet Street.

Left: *James 'Gunner' Moir was knocked out in the tenth round when challenging for the heavyweight boxing championship of the world in 1907. The holder, Tommy Burns, successfully defended his title twelve times in less than two years.*

publications, was the creation of the diminutive John Wisden (1826–84), who organised the first English tour of North America, in one match taking six wickets in successive balls. In 1850, playing for 'the North', he clean bowled the entire batting order of 'the South'. After coaching at Harrow, Wisden took over a Sussex pub (named, inevitably, the Cricketers), opened a West End shop selling cricket gear and cigars, and in 1864 published the first annual edition of his *Almanac*, which included the results of classic horse races, the rules of quoits, useful facts about canals and coinage, and a short history of China. Cricketers' births and deaths were recorded from 1867, descriptions of matches from 1870.

A sporting literature continued to develop in parallel with the expansion of the sporting press. In 1868 the novelist Anthony Trollope, a keen huntsman, published a survey of *British Sports and Pastimes*. More typical was the sort of rambling memoir represented by Sir John Astley's *Fifty Years of My Life in the World of Sport*. More useful was the sporting manual devoted to technique, such as H. G. Hutchinson's highly successful *Hints on the Game of Golf* (1886) and the pioneering work (1906) of the Japanese master Yukio Tani, *The Game of Ju-Jitsu: for the Use of Schools and Colleges*.

A brilliant Oxford classics scholar, Charles Burgess Fry (1872–1956) held the world record for the long jump, played in twenty-six Test matches, was the first county player to hit six centuries in successive innings, six times topped the annual batting averages and played for Southampton in an FA Cup Final. Fry also compiled landmark books on batting and bowling technique, illustrated with photographs. In later life a prolific sporting journalist, Fry pioneered a novel genre by interviewing professional sportsmen for their insider's perspective.

SPORT FOR ALL?

Although female children played ball games and traditional holidays in rural areas had often included running races for girls, and although there were women who rode and even rode to hounds, almost the only sport as such practised by women in the early nineteenth century was archery. For the more daring there was skating in the winter. Croquet came in as a social pastime for both sexes from the 1850s until it gave way to the tennis craze in the 1870s and, for the more adventurous, cycling in the 1890s. That said, a golf match for the town's fishwives was organised by Musselburgh Golf Club as early as 1811 and in the same year a team of Surrey women played a team of Hampshire women at cricket. The St Andrews Ladies Golf Club was founded in 1867. As golf spread south of the border from the 1880s this was followed by the formation of the Ladies' Golf Union in 1893.

Largely as a by-product of the expansion of more formal and more demanding educational provision, led by elite institutions such as Cheltenham Ladies' College and North London Collegiate School, sporting opportunities for females became more diverse, more demanding and more competitive. Roedean girls were expected to do two hours sport or exercise daily in winter, three in summer. With their modesty protected from the male gaze by secluded surroundings, girls could engage in far more vigorous

Left: *Long before women were expected to participate in sport, they were valued as appreciative, if often uncomprehending, spectators before whom male prowess could be displayed. As a Frenchman, the artist Gustave Doré might perhaps have been expected to be indifferent to cricket as a game but he was clearly fascinated with Lord's as a venue. Society beauties, dressed in the height of fashion, figure prominently in the crowd – as they did on such occasions as the Eton v Harrow and Gentlemen v Players matches, when male spectators brought their sisters and sisters brought their friends to one of the largest concentrations of eligible young males the capital could offer.*

PRACTISING FOR A MATCH.

Leonora. "DEAR! DEAR! HOW THE ARROW STICKS!"
Capt. Blank. (with a sigh of the deepest). "IT DOES, INDEED!"

Above right: *Archery's leisurely pace and limited demand for exertion made it one of the few sports judged suitable for both sexes. As such, it provided an occasion for socialising and courtship, as suggested in this cartoon of 1862 by John Leech.*

Right: *Archery as a social pastime was largely swept away by tennis in the 1870s, leaving devotees to pursue it as a serious competitive sport, as seen at this meeting of the Toxophilite Society in Regent's Park in 1894. In 1908 Queenie Newall won the archery to become the oldest Olympic champion to date, and for decades to come, at the age of fifty-three.*

Croquet was quite compatible with voluminous and constricting female fashions and its leisurely pace offered ample opportunities for courtship. The joke illustrated depends on a pun on the word 'spooning'. First recorded in 1831 as a slang term for silly or sentimental flirtation, it was recorded in 1865 as a technical term for pushing a ball without an audible knock. The cartoonist was therefore exploiting a very recent coinage.

SWEET DELUSION.—*Chorus of Young Ladies (speaking technically).* "No *spooning*, Mr. Lovel! No *spooning* allowed here!" *Miss Tabitha (with the long curls).* "Those naughty, n-n-naughty girls! I suppose they allude to you and me, Mr. Lovel. But, lor'! never mind them!—*I* don't."

activities, involving both perspiration and physical contact. Hockey, lacrosse and netball soon became established as favoured female sports although athletics and swimming were hindered by the issue of modesty. An English Lacrosse Association was founded as early as 1868, only a year after one had been formed in Canada, from where this highly hazardous sport had been imported. The All England Women's Hockey Association, by contrast, was not formed until 1891. In 1896 the scholarly Dr Frederick Furnivall founded a Sculling Club for Girls at Hammersmith, the members being factory hands, café waitresses and Harrod's sales assistants.

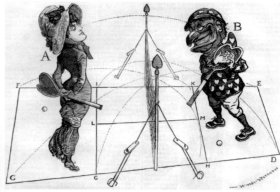

Above: *Geometry of passion. Heart-shaped motifs abound in this cartoon of 1879 by the masterly Linley Sambourne. Like croquet, lawn tennis rapidly established itself as an eminently suitable occasion for suburban courtship.*

Left: *Bovril was one of the earliest food products to try to capitalise on an association with health. Note the golf-bag at bottom right.*

A rather fanciful depiction of Lottie Dod. Her youth enabled her to wear a cricketer's cap and rather shorter skirts than shown here, possibly giving her some edge over opponents more cumbrously attired.

The most outstanding sportswoman of the era was Charlotte ('Lottie') Dod (1871–1960), five times Wimbledon singles champion, who also played hockey for England, won the British Women's Golf Championship and a silver medal for archery at the 1908 Olympics and excelled at mountaineering, skating, riding, sculling and billiards.

The emergence of physical education as a discipline was primarily the result of foreign influences. Gymnastic exercise was first systematised in Scandinavia and Germany. In 1885 the imperious Martina Bergman-Osterberg (1849–1915), inventor of both the gymslip and, in effect, the games mistress, established the first physical training college in Hampstead, moving it to Dartford in 1905. Severely elitist in social as well as sporting terms, she never envisaged either physical education or team games having much role in mass education. She was largely right. In the new 'board schools' which appeared from 1870 onwards, exercise was largely limited to repetitive paramilitary 'drill', which required no

A lengthy caption accompanying this depiction of a ladies' doubles match in 1879 suggests sending British players to France as a gesture of reciprocity for the number of French actresses sent to Britain. The Francophile artist George du Maurier had studied in Paris. The costumes of the players and the top-hatted nature of the crowd imply the elevated social standing of all concerned. Note the aprons worn by the players over high-fashion day dresses.

Jules Léotard (1830–70) invented both the flying trapeze and the close-fitting costume named after him. The son of a French army physical training instructor, Léotard abandoned the study of law to make his name at the Alhambra, Leicester Square, for the fabulous sum of £180 a week and inspired George Leybourne, the original 'Champagne Charlie', to compose 'The Daring Young Man on the Flying Trapeze' in his honour. Although gymnastics had been developed as a scientifically based activity in Scandinavia and Germany a quarter of a century earlier, in mid-Victorian Britain it was still associated with the circus strong-man and stage tumbler.

specialised equipment, could be performed in an asphalt yard or school hall and was often supervised by ex-army instructors paid a few pence by the hour. The appalling revelations of the unfitness of volunteers for service in the second Boer War (1899–1902), only two in nine of whom were judged fully fit for combat service, led to top-level government initiatives in pursuit of 'national efficiency' – school meals, medical inspections and the promotion of more scientifically based 'Swedish drill'. Painfully impressed by Boer standards of marksmanship, the nation's favourite soldier, Earl Roberts of Kandahar VC campaigned to have shooting introduced in the public schools. Sport at last became an official part of the curriculum of elementary schools from 1906 onwards.

An Edwardian girls' physical education class at an Islington board school. Exercising with barbells was supposed to develop good posture and a graceful carriage in walking. Is the lurking figure in uniform (centre rear) supervising or spectating?

As the caption to this 1839 picture of Regent's Park makes clear, ice-skating provided the occasion for a display of winter fashions. In the Netherlands the existence of extensive canals made speed skating popular but Britons, limited to park lakes and ponds, concentrated on elaborating the art of figure skating.

THE SPORTING SETTING

The multiple pressures of diversification, codification, commercialisation and mass participation combined to favour investment in more extensive, better-equipped and more specialised sporting facilities.

An outdoor gymnasium was established in Regent's Park in 1825 by Carl Voelke and another is shown on the north-eastern edge of Bloomsbury on Greenwood's London map of 1827. The first purpose-built gymnasium was constructed at the East India Company College, Addiscombe, Surrey, in 1851. Uppingham was the first school to erect a gymnasium, in 1859. In 1865 the Turnhalle, a state-of-the-art exercise complex, was opened at St Pancras by the recently founded Turnverein (German Gymnastic Society).

Eton had the first recorded cricket practice nets in 1839 and built its first fives court in 1840. At Harrow School the playing-fields, which covered 8 acres (3.2 hectares) in 1845, were extended to 146 acres (59 hectares) by 1900. St Paul's, Merchant Taylors'

The text accompanying this illustration of salmon fishing in 1870 noted that anglers were travelling to Ireland and Norway in search of more challenging sport. It also asserted that the sport was ideal for 'the old gentleman in our picture', who was past the exertions of foxhunting but still possessed the 'skill and patience' essential for landing the wily salmon.

35

With a gallery for an orchestra, the Chelsea Glaciarium was clearly intended for skaters who favoured elegance over exertion. Note the avant-garde Japanese décor.

and Charterhouse all moved out of the City of London to gain access to more extensive grounds. Harrow built the earliest known squash courts in 1864 and in 1866 installed a concrete-sided swimming pool. From 1869 Powderhall Park, Edinburgh, became the premier venue for professional sprint races.

Chelsea had the dual distinction of accommodating the Glaciarium indoor ice-rink, which opened in 1876, and hosting the first indoor athletics meeting, at the Ashbourne Hall. Less happily, in 1887 its celebrated athletics ground at Lillie Bridge was burned down by a mob enraged by a match-fixing scandal when two professional sprinters failed to agree on who should lose.

The first golf course for English players, rather than for Scottish exiles, was opened at Westward Ho!, Devon, in 1864. A second London course opened at Wimbledon in 1865. The collapse of agricultural prices and rents from the 1870s onwards greatly cheapened the cost of the hundred or so acres needed for a course and by 1914 over a thousand had been laid out. The same factor applied to tennis clubs, whose number rose

This cartoon of 1889 clearly implies that golf was still unfamiliar to most people south of the Scottish border. Note the caddies holding loose clubs, the golf-bag not having yet come into general use.

The ritualised shoots of East Anglia offered sportsmen the chance to test their skills on intensively reared pheasants and partridges. Grouse, by contrast, were to be sought on the heather moors that were their natural habitat.

from some three hundred in 1900 to a thousand by 1914.

In 1875 Sandown Park opened as the first enclosed racecourse, making it possible to charge admission to the ground and not just the stand. Enclosure also made it possible for stewards to banish the boxing booths and other unseemly attractions that had traditionally attached themselves to race meetings. London's first cycle track opened at Paddington in 1888. Herne Hill stadium opened as the first purpose-built velodrome in 1891. Cycling was so popular in the north-east of England that tracks were laid out within a few miles of each other at Wallsend, Jarrow and Gateshead.

What became the standard form of the football stadium was devised by the Glasgow engineer Archibald Leith and consisted of a rectangle with a two-tier grandstand along one of the long sides, the other three sides being single-tiered and open to the elements. Between 1889 and 1910 fifty-eight professional clubs moved into new grounds. In 1907 English rugby found a 10 acre (4 hectare) home out at suburban Twickenham on what had been known locally as 'Billy Williams' Cabbage Patch'.

As municipal authorities became accountable to a broader electorate with the extension of the franchise to working men, they began to provide sporting facilities such as cricket pitches, tennis courts, bowling greens and swimming baths. Birmingham, a

Boxing booths in which experienced, often aging, professionals took on all comers were a common feature of travelling fairs. These opponents, shown in 1872, are wearing gloves, although these did not become universal until the 1890s.

Bowls lost much of its popularity in the mid nineteenth century but was revived from its Scottish heartland, encouraged by the provision of greens in public parks, as shown here, in the 1890s.

self-consciously progressive city, opened its Burbery Street Recreation Ground in 1877. It was noted as early as 1879 that Victoria Park in London's East End, the first park purposely created for the working classes, 'differs from the West End parks in being supplied with various appliances for amusement'. These included bathing lakes, tennis courts, cricket nets, an athletic track, a bowling green and an 'outdoor gymnasium'. Enlightened employers like Cadbury, the Quaker chocolate manufacturers, likewise provided the inhabitants of their model housing estates with cricket pitches, bowling greens and tennis courts. Although public houses could not compete in terms of scale or sophistication, many continued to have skittle alleys, bowling greens, billiards tables and dart boards, all of which provided opportunities for betting, which would be prohibited at municipal facilities.

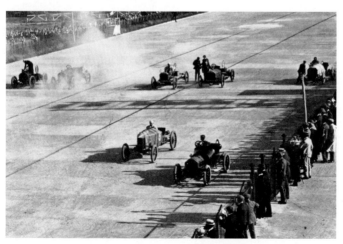

The start of a relay race at Brooklands in 1909. Built of ferro-concrete in 1906–7, Brooklands was the world's first purpose-built motor-racing circuit.

THE OLYMPIC IDEAL

The revival of Olympianism was the work of a French aristocrat, Baron Pierre de Coubertin (1863–1937), who, deeply impressed by the British public school and the global spread of British games, saw in sport a means of bringing nations closer together. The first modern Olympiad, hosted by Athens in 1896, was poorly organised but enthusiastically received. The second was muddled up with the Paris Exposition of 1900. Travel distances meant that the third, in St Louis, Missouri, in 1904, was virtually an all-American affair.

The 1908 Olympiad was scheduled for Italy but the eruption of Mount Vesuvius in 1906 forced the intended host to focus on reconstruction. Britain stepped in, despite having neither venue nor budget. The world's first purpose-built Olympic stadium, complete with swimming tank and banked cycle track, was erected in record time next to the White City exhibition centre at Shepherd's Bush. Fifteen hundred athletes from nineteen nations competed before 300,000 spectators. For the first time the administration of the games was in the hands of experienced officials, although there were still accusations of biased judging. Important innovations included the first 'winter' event – ice-skating; the first javelin contest; the awarding of silver and bronze medals; the production of an official report; and the establishment of a definitive distance for the marathon at 26 miles 385 yards (42.195 km). Britain won more medals than all the other contestants added together – which seems a positive note to end on.

Above left: *Charlotte Cooper was the first female Olympic champion, winning the women's singles tennis at the 1900 Paris games. She also won the women's singles at Wimbledon five times between 1895 and 1908.*

Above right: *George Larner winning the 3500 metre walk at the 1908 London Olympics, the only occasion on which this event was held. Larner, a Brighton policeman, also won the 10 mile walk and in 1909 published a textbook on walking as both a sport and a mode of exercise. Habitually training barefoot, Larner also recommended running circuits naked in a secluded garden, preferably in the rain.*

FURTHER READING

Arlott, J. (editor). *The Oxford Companion to Sports and Games.* Oxford University Press, 1976.
Birley, D. *A Social History of English Cricket.* Aurum, 1999.
Brailsford, D. *Bareknuckles: A Social History of Prizefighting.* Lutterworth Press, 1988.
Dunning, E., and Sheard, K. *Barbarians, Gentlemen and Players.* Martin Robertson, 1979.
Fletcher, S. *Women First: The Female Tradition in English Physical Education 1880–1980.* Athlone Press, 1984.
Holt, R. *Sport and the British: A Modern History.* Oxford University Press, 1990.
Holt, R. (editor). *Sport and the Working Classes in Modern Britain.* Manchester University Press, 1990.
Itzkowitz, D. C. *Peculiar Privilege: A Social History of English Fox Hunting.* Harvester Press, 1977.
Lowerson, J. *Sport and the English Middle Classes 1870–1914.* Manchester University Press, 1993.
Mangan, J. A. *Athleticism in the Victorian and Edwardian Public School: The Emergence and Consolidation of the Educational Ideology.* Cambridge University Press, 1981.
Mangan, J. A. *Pleasure, Profit, Proselytism: British Culture and Sport at Home and Abroad 1700–1914.* Cass, 1988.
Mason, T. *Association Football and English Society 1863–1915.* Harvester Press, 1980.
Money, T. *Manly and Muscular Diversions: Public Schools and the Nineteenth Century Sporting Revival.* Duckworth, 1997.
Penn, A. *Targeting Schools: Drill, Militarism and Imperialism.* Woburn Press, 1999.
Sandiford, K. *Cricket and the Victorians.* Scolar Press, 1994.
Sissons, R. *The Players: A Social History of the Professional Cricketer.* Kingswood, 1988.
Sutherland, D. *The Mad Hatters: Great Sporting Eccentrics of the Nineteenth Century.* Robert Hale, 1987.
Tames, R. *Sporting London: A Race through Time.* Historical Publications, 2005.
Tranter, N. *Sport, Economy and Society in Britain 1750–1914.* Cambridge University Press, 1988.
Vamplew, W. *Pay Up and Play the Game: Professional Sport in Britain 1875–1914.* Cambridge University Press, 1988.
Walker, S. A. *Sporting Art: England 1700–1900.* Studio Vista, 1972.

PLACES TO VISIT

To avoid disappointment, intending visitors are advised to check the times and dates of opening before travelling.

Belmont House and Garden, Belmont Park, Throwley, Faversham, Kent ME13 0HH. Telephone: 01795 890202. Website: www.belmont-house.org (Associations with the fourth Lord Harris, distinguished cricketer.)
The British Golf Museum, Bruce Embankment, St Andrews, Fife KY16 9AB. Telephone: 01334 460046. Website: www.britishgolfmuseum.co.uk
Brooklands Museum, Brooklands Road, Weybridge, Surrey KT13 0QN. Telephone: 01932 857381. Website: www.brooklandsmuseum.com
Dick Galloway Archery Museum, Scottish Archery Centre, Fenton Barns, North Berwick, East Lothian EH39 5BW. Telephone: 01620 850401. Website: www.scottisharcherycentre.co.uk
The MCC Museum, Lord's Ground, St John's Wood, London NW8 8QN. Telephone: 020 7616 8595 or 8596. Website: www.mcc.org.uk/history/mcc-museum
The Museum of Rugby, Twickenham Stadium, Rugby Road, Twickenham, Middlesex TW1 1DZ. Telephone: 0870 405 2001. Website: www.rfu.com/microsites/museum/index.cfm
The National Cycle Collection, The Automobile Palace, Temple Street, Llandrindod Wells, Powys LD1 5DL. Telephone: 01597 825531. Website: www.cyclemuseum.org.uk
The National Football Museum, Sir Tom Finney Way, Deepdale, Preston, Lancashire PR1 6RU. Telephone: 01772 908442. Website: www.nationalfootballmuseum.com
The National Horseracing Museum, 99 High Street, Newmarket, Suffolk CB8 8JH. Telephone: 01638 667333. Website: www.nhrm.co.uk
River and Rowing Museum, Mill Meadows, Henley-on-Thames, Oxfordshire RG9 1BF. Telephone: 01491 415600. Website: www.rrm.co.uk
Wimbledon Lawn Tennis Museum, Church Road, Wimbledon, London SW19 5AE. Telephone: 020 8946 6131. Website: www.wimbledon.org/museum